ALCATRAZ
Bride

At Home on the Rock

◇◇

by
Ann Burrows Eib

GOLDEN GATE NATIONAL PARKS CONSERVANCY
SAN FRANCISCO, CALIFORNIA

Unless otherwise noted, all photographs and memorabilia are from the author's personal collection. Most are protected by copyright and/or require permission to reproduce.

Collier's (August 6, 1954): pp. 24, 30

Phil Dollison Collection: p. 72

Golden Gate National Recreation Area/Park Archives and Records Center (PARC): pp. 2, 5, 10, 12, 14, 15 (bottom), 17 (top, Joseph H. Simpson Collection, bottom, Fred Straley Collection), 25 (bottom), 31 (bottom), 34, 39, 40-41, 75

PARC/Don Bowden Collection: pp. 11 (bottom), 15 (top), 16 (bottom), 18-19 (top), 25 (top), 31 (top)

San Francisco Chronicle: Cover and pp. 55 (bottom), 57, 59/ Ken McLaughlin; p. 66/Joe Rosenthal

San Francisco Public Library: pp. 32-33 (top), 62

Spot illustrations: Vivian Young

Library of Congress Control Number: 2011920532
ISBN 978-1-932519-15-0

Development: Robert Lieber
Design: Vivian Young
Editor: Susan Tasaki
Production: Sarah Lau

Printed in Hong Kong

PARKS FOR ALL FOREVER™

Acknowledgments

I'd like to thank the following for their support: my daughters, Karen E. January and Sharrie Ann Eskina; my son, Michael Conner, and his wife, Annette Conner; my friend, Phil Dollison; and the Alcatraz Alumni Association *(www.alcatrazalumniassoc.org).* I would also like to thank Kathleen Knoblock, project designer and editor for the first edition of this book.

Me watching TV in our Alcatraz living room

Introduction

My name is Ann Burrows Eib, and during the 1950s, I spent almost three years on Alcatraz—not as an inmate, but as a teenager whose father was a guard at the prison. Over the years, I have found that, although most people know a good bit about Alcatraz, few know that families actually lived there, in the shadow of a prison building that housed almost three hundred of the nation's hardest criminals.

I lived on Alcatraz between the ages of fifteen and seventeen. As a normal young girl, I thought about and cared about the same things as most girls my age: fashion, friends, and boys! Like teen girls everywhere, my on-island friends and I saw what others were wearing, checked out the latest fashions in local department stores, talked about clothes and trends with other kids, and were influenced by what we saw on television. I subscribed to *Seventeen*, one of my favorite magazines. My curiosity about the inmates had little to do with why they were there or what they had done, but rather, whether they were cute!

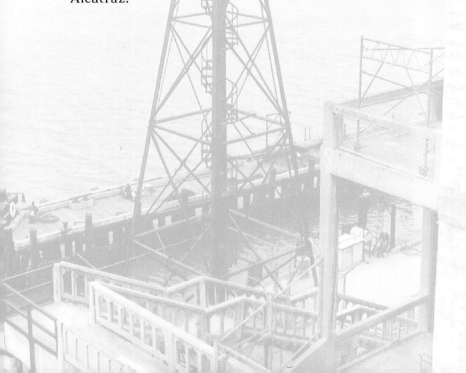

Yes, a lot has been written about Alcatraz—the military years, the inmates, the prison. Though the Department of Justice closed the island prison more than forty years ago, people continue to be captivated by its stories. But soon, there'll be no one left to relate first-hand accounts of what it was like back in its heyday. I was there and, if my experiences and those of others who lived on the island are not preserved, they will be lost forever. This book was written not just to satisfy the curious, but also to share my story—a small contribution to the preservation of the legacy of Alcatraz.

Moving to Alcatraz

Kansas City, Missouri, January 1955

The holidays were over and I was anxious to get back to school. Not that I didn't enjoy Christmas vacation, but I missed my friends and school activities.

For the first fifteen years, my life was completely ordinary. I was born in a small town in southern Missouri, and my parents moved to Kansas City when I was a baby. I had an older brother, Ronald. My father, William Burrows (Bill), was employed at the Federal Reserve Bank of Kansas City, and my Uncle John (Dad's brother, John Burrows) worked as a guard at US Penitentiary Leavenworth, Kansas. Since Leavenworth was only thirty miles away, we often got together with my uncle and his family to catch up on family news.

My father and uncle had been discussing Alcatraz for some time. When my uncle found out that Alcatraz needed guards, he applied. Once his request for transfer was accepted, we knew he and his family would soon be leaving for Alcatraz.

My father decided to apply for employment at the

prison as well, and was hired. After he resigned his position at the bank, we moved to Leavenworth, where Dad would work until the transfer came through. Then we'd all be going to Alcatraz!

The news came a surprise, but it didn't really upset me; my family often visited Uncle John's family in Leavenworth, so I knew a little bit about the area. But I would have to change schools mid-year and then again when my father's reassignment to Alcatraz came through.

I knew about Leavenworth, but I'd never heard of Alcatraz. When my parents told me we'd be moving there, my first question was, "Where's that?" My mother and I went to the library and found as much information as we could.

Some kids in my position might have felt apprehensive, but I looked forward to it. Though I was a bit dismayed about leaving my friends, I really didn't have any other concerns because I was about to embark on an exciting new adventure.

When my homeroom teacher announced to the class that I was moving to Alcatraz, we had a lively discussion. The teacher took time to tell everyone about Alcatraz and its history, and the kids treated me

like it was something very special; they were full of
questions. I got a lot of attention from my classmates,
and all my friends wanted me to write to them.

The more I learned about Alcatraz, the more able
I was to imagine what it would be like to live there.
Because Alcatraz is an island near the Pacific
Ocean, I pictured myself sunbathing, washed in
warm sea breezes. Obviously, I had not yet learned
that "island near the Pacific" does not necessarily
mean "warm and sunny"!

Welcome to California

Our apartment

Arrival

San Francisco, California, 1955

When his transfer came though, Dad decided to make the trip a vacation. We piled in our old Nash Rambler and spent about two-and-a-half weeks on Route 66 getting to California. Arriving on Alcatraz was the last stop in what I thought of as a long adventure.

Once we got to San Francisco, instead of going straight to Alcatraz, we had to live on the mainland until quarters on the island became available. For a few months, we had an apartment in the city; then, finally, my dad was notified that an apartment was available. Off we went again.

We arrived on Alcatraz on the *Warden Johnston*, a vessel I would come to know very well. As we approached the island, the first thing I saw, of course, was the dock. When we disembarked, I also saw seven or eight men dressed in khaki pants and shirts lined up on a yellow line on the dock. I soon learned they were well-supervised inmates who were given work assignments in the dock area. We signed in and resident guards showed us around the island, then took us to our quarters.

We entered our apartment through a large sun porch that led into the living room, which had a large corner fireplace and two windows overlooking the bay. From our windows we could see Oakland and the Oakland Bay Bridge. There were also three bedrooms, a kitchen, and hardwood floors throughout.

About half of the island was set aside for resident employees and their families. In this area, nothing was fenced in except the prison side and forbidden areas close to the prison walls. We could see the prisoners, especially those working on the dock. The inmates were supervised, but there was no special supervision for the kids, who were free to come and go within the family compound.

On my first night on the island, we attended a movie—*I'll Cry Tomorrow*, with Susan Hayward. During intermission, several girls about my age introduced themselves to me. They were very nice, and friendly, and although we had just met, they made me feel like I had always known them. It just so happened that they were having a slumber party that night, and I was pleased to be invited.

View from our apartment building

prison building

lighthouse

warden's house

When the movie was over, we went to my apartment to get my pajamas and then to my new girlfriend's apartment. She lived what seemed like far away in one of the newer apartments across the parade ground. We had a lot of fun talking and getting acquainted on the way.

Our back yard

Roadway to the top of the island—the last of the wooden houses on the left was destroyed by fire during the Indian occupation.

Settling In

Alcatraz Island, 1955

The Bureau of Prisons provided the quarters and its furnishings. My parents brought my bed—a nice double bed with a bookcase headboard—and our television, which required a converter to run on the island's DC current. My parents also opted to bring their living room set, coffee table, and end tables. Everything came to the island on a barge. Once we settled in, it felt like home.

More than one hundred families lived on Alcatraz at the time—from childless couples to parents with children infant through college age. There were plenty of kids, enough that it was easy to make friends; at fifteen, I had no trouble finding people my age to hang out with.

There was a store on the island that we called the canteen, and we were able to find just about all the groceries we needed there (clothing, furniture, linens, and things of that sort had to be purchased on the mainland). The store even had a butcher—one of the

Canteen soda fountain

Supplies arriving at the dock

The canteen

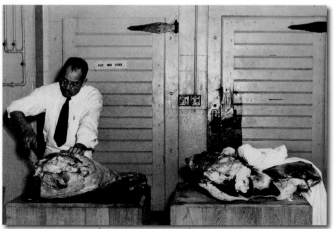

Butcher at work in the prison kitchen

Flowers from the island's gardens

our window looking Bay

guards—so we were also able to get fresh meat. The guards took turns working in the canteen.

In addition to the on-site store, there was a big social, or community, hall for the families. It was more than just a place to meet, though. Activities were provided for our enjoyment—from a two-lane bowling alley and ping-pong tables to a soda fountain. We even had a former Arthur Murray dance instructor who came to the island once a week and gave lessons. At the social hall, ladies held their club meetings, kids and families enjoyed group activities, and people got

Ron, 1956

together for all kinds of reasons. The social hall was the center of the community and the focal point of the families' lives.

My brother Ron was two-and-a-half years older than me and had graduated from high school by the time we moved to the island. He was employed by General Electric, where he worked until he joined the military. He did, however, live on the island with us on and off through the years. Ron, who was a bookworm, had a girlfriend on the island; when he wasn't working, he mostly hung out with her. Of course, there was always television to watch during his free time.

I was much more of a social butterfly. Whenever I could, I headed over to the canteen to see if my friends were there, and they usually were. We'd get sodas and sit around talking.

Mom at front door, which opened into sun porch

My mother, Vida, belonged to the Ladies' Club. She participated in all the activities, such as the recipe exchange, sewing circles, and so on. Mom also frequently went to the city to shop and do errands. We had relatives in Oakland whom she sometimes visited, and occasionally, they came to the island to see us. Though she later got a job at the Bank of America, she stayed active in the Ladies' Club.

Not all of the guards lived on the island; some had homes on the mainland and preferred it that way. Dad didn't want to live in the city;

Meetings

Regualr meeting shall be held on the third Monday of each month.

Membership

The Women of the Officer's family.

Dues

Twenty five cents per month or two dollars and fifty cents per year.

March 19th, 1956

Hostesses:

    Hazel Dolby

    Eunice Inman

    Doris Moore

April 16th, 1956

Hostesses:

    Marjorie Hack

    Margaret McCreary

    Eileen Mitchell

Minutes of Alcatraz Women's Club meeting, 1956

Mom in our apartment

CITIZEN

No. 1450192c

STATE OF
CALIFORNIA

$**3**.00

RESIDENT
CITIZEN

ANGLING
LICENSE

EXPIRES
DEC. 31, 1956

Name W. G. BURROWS
Street Address ALCATRAZ ISLAND
City SAN FRANCISCO
Age 41 Height 5 Ft. 11 In. Weight 165
Eyes BRN Hair BRN Sex M
I am a citizen of the U.S.A. and have resided in California for the past six (6) months.

Signature X Wm Burrows
Date Issued 9-23-56
Issued by MUNY BAIT SHOP

Dad (left) and a friend
with their shark catch

he would have had to drive to the dock, wait on the pier to catch the boat, and then take the bay ride to work. Then, at the end of the day, do it all again. It was much more convenient (and more interesting) to live on the island.

Both my family and my Uncle John and Aunt Ilene lived in Building 64; my aunt and uncle had an apartment on the lower balcony, while ours was on the upper balcony and to the side. Mom and Aunt Ilene visited back and forth, and my dad and uncle were always doing something together. Dad also enjoyed fishing off of the dock with his friends; he and another guard once caught a leopard shark.

Eating together was a family event. We had family dinners at home, but we also ate out two or three times a week. We didn't have family barbeques on the island, but we enjoyed them when we visited relatives on the mainland.

Though people who lived on the mainland depended on cars to get to work, shopping, and entertainment, we had no need for them while we were on the island. Personal cars couldn't be brought on to Alcatraz, so most of the families who lived there kept their vehicles in rented garages in San Francisco. That's what my father decided to do with ours. When the family went to the mainland, we would leave Alcatraz on the *Warden Johnston*, arrive at the Fort Mason dock, then walk two or three blocks to the garage where Dad kept our car.

In the closed environment of Alcatraz, families spent a lot of time with both one another and with other families. In many ways, the island felt like one big family. We soon learned that if anyone needed help, someone was always there; everyone helped one another.

The soda fountain in the basement of the social hall was another favorite meeting place

Watching the boat leave

Laundry day, Building 64 apartments

Leaving Alcatraz

Weekly	Saturday	Sunday	Holiday
A.M.	A.M.	A.M.	A.M.
12:15	12:15	12:15	12:15
6:45	7:00	7:00	7:00
7:20			
8:10	8:10	8:10	8:10
10:00	10:00	10:00	10:00
P.M.	P.M.	P.M.	P.M.
12:45	12:45	12:45	12:45
3:25	3:25	3:25	3:25
5:00	5:00	5:00	5:00
5:40	5:40	5:40	5:40
7:00	7:00	7:00	7:00
10:00	10:00	10:00	10:00
11:15	11:15	11:15	11:15

(Reverse Side Leaving Ft. Mason)

BOAT SCHEDULE

Leaving Ft. Mason

Weekly	Saturday	Sunday	Holiday
A.M.	A.M.	A.M.	A.M.
12:25	12:25	12:25	12:25
6:55	7:10	7:10	7:10
7:30			
8:20	8:20	8:20	8:20
10:10	10:10	10:10	10:10
P.M.	P.M.	P.M.	P.M.
12:55	12:55	12:55	12:55
3:35	3:35	3:35	3:35
5:10	5:10	5:10	5:10
5:50	5:50	5:50	5:50
7:15	7:15	7:15	7:15
10:15	10:15	10:15	10:15
11:30	11:30	11:30	11:30

(Reverse Side Leaving Alcatraz)

Aunt Ilene and I aboard the Warden Johnston, headed to the mainland for a shopping trip

Life on Alcatraz

1955-1956

Although much about life on Alcatraz was just like anywhere else, it was unique in some ways. Many things that were taken for granted in other communities were unavailable to us, and we had to adjust accordingly.

The canteen had newspapers and magazines, but the selection was limited. Supplies, paper goods, shampoo—the canteen had all those things as well, but again, there weren't many choices. For the things we couldn't buy on the island, we caught the boat to the mainland and did our shopping there.

There was no bank and no barbershop. No pharmacy or department store. There was no movie theater, but the social hall was equipped to show movies, which they did once a week. These were billed as first-run films, but they had been censored because they were also shown to the inmates.

When something broke down and needed repair, there was no corner plumber or handyman. The inmates were called upon to do some of this work, and when they couldn't, someone from the city had to come over—escorted, of course—to fix things.

Everyone went about their business, doing things people did everywhere. To us, living by a boat schedule was no different than living by a bus schedule like people in the city did. We just had to adjust to the fact that not everything we wanted or needed was readily available—many things required planning. The fact that there was no mall, no supermarket, no baseball park, no skating rink, no library, and no bars or restaurants made us a closer-knit community. Despite the lack of options, or perhaps because of them, we made our own fun.

My friends and I came up with creative things to do. For example, when the tides went out, we would take a homemade spear—a stick with a point on it—go to the dock, and gig starfish. We'd put them in salt and set them in the sun to dry out, then paint them. We also took walks, usually to the beach near the cottages. The shoreline was covered with small rocks; sometimes we'd turn over the rocks, which disturbed the small crabs hiding under them, and watch the crabs run for cover.

Holidays were special. One Halloween, Aunt Ilene

and I dressed up like witches. After making sure no one would recognize us, we went around the island trick-or-treating—mainly to our friends' houses. We had to tell them who we were, and we all got a big laugh out of it. The Ladies' Club also planned an evening Halloween party for us. There was always quite an array of holiday activities staged for us, and they were always fun.

◇◇◇◇◇◇◇◇◇◇◇◇◇◇◇◇◇◇◇◇◇◇◇◇◇◇

Along with everything else we didn't have on Alcatraz, there was no school; we went to school in San Francisco. By the time my family moved to Alcatraz, I had missed a lot of class time, so for the rest of that year, I was tutored, which also involved trips to the mainland.

Especially at the high-school level, many social activities are tied to school, and it was important to be involved in all aspects of school life. Despite our physical separation from the city, we were able take part in just about everything.

Though teenagers can be hard on people who are different, all of us who lived on Alcatraz found that rather than being treated as "outsiders" as some might expect, we were the subjects of curiosity—the other

Off to school

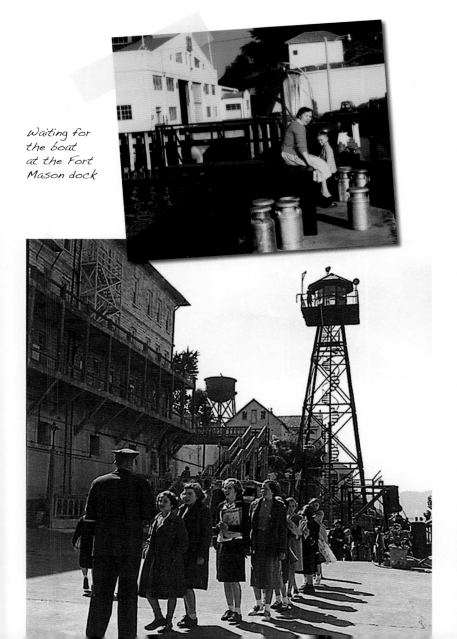

Waiting for the boat at the Fort Mason dock

San Francisco, looking toward the
Golden Gate Bridge

Palace of Fine Arts,
in the Marina area

View of Alcatraz from the city

Most of the people who lived on the
island went to town frequently, for
a variety of reasons—shopping, seeing
friends, eating out, going to the doctor
or dentist, to see a concert, and so on.

Dock guard tower, where the keys to the launch were kept

kids were interested in and inquisitive about our unusual circumstances. Then, and now, people just wanted to know what it was like.

My life as a teenager on Alcatraz was very much the same as that of teenagers everywhere. I did homework, watched television, had friends over, and sometimes, got in trouble with my parents. Because there were a lot of pretty scary men sharing the island with us, there were a few extra rules, but for the most part, I was free to live as a normal teen.

The inmates, of course, were monitored, but we weren't. We all came and went as we pleased in the

View from our
apartment—
Treasure Island
and the Bay
Bridge

family section of the island, or back and forth to the mainland. Of course, our parents dictated our comings and goings, but those were our only restrictions. The families on Alcatraz knew a lot of families who lived in the city, and our parents made sure that we had their addresses and phone numbers. If we somehow missed the last boat, we called them, they picked us up, and we stayed overnight at their house.

For a teenager—and everyone else who lived on Alcatraz—life revolved around the boat schedule. The boat between the island and the city started running about 4:45 or 5 a.m., and the last boat back to island left the mainland dock around midnight or a little after. We not only went back and forth every day for school, most of the people who lived on the island went to town frequently, for a variety of reasons—shopping, seeing friends, eating out, going to the doctor or dentist, to see a concert, and so on.

I was invited to the senior prom by one of the boys on the island, and we went with another couple, boarding the *Warden Johnston* in our formal wear. We went to Fisherman's Wharf for dinner and then to the prom. And a bit like Cinderella, just before the stroke of midnight, we hurried to catch the boat home.

We were not allowed on the dock when the inmates were out on work assignments, except when it was almost time to board the boat. Near boarding time, a horn was blown, a signal to the inmates to line up on the yellow line on the dock; two guards stayed with them until the boat left. The keys to the boat were kept in the dock guard tower and were lowered to the pilot when he was ready to go. On return trips, the keys went back up on the pulley as soon as the boat docked.

Although the *Warden Johnston* was the main transport, there was a back-up, the *McDowell*, named after Fort McDowell on Angel Island. The *McDowell* was a little slower than the *Warden Johnston*—taking forty-

The McDowell

five minutes instead of thirty to get to the mainland—
but the price was right: all rides to and from the island
were free!

◇◇◇◇◇◇◇◇◇◇◇◇◇◇◇◇◇◇◇◇◇◇◇◇◇◇

Normal, I suppose, is what you're used to. In that
regard, living on Alcatraz felt normal to me. Still,
there were several things that people who lived in San
Francisco (or anywhere but Alcatraz) would no doubt
have considered not normal.

For example, unlike "normal" cities, Alcatraz was
basically self-contained. Almost everything that was
needed was provided, and almost everything that
needed to be done was done by a "built-in" work force.
This gave life on the island some advantages. For

example, the prison had its own factories and facilities, including a complete laundry. The prisoners did a lot of the mundane tasks not just for the prison, but for everyone. Every day, a small group of heavily guarded prisoners moved around the island, working at the dock, trimming the trees, and cleaning up around the buildings. They collected our trash every morning, and they also came once a week to pick up our laundry, which we put out in a designated area. They came and got it and then returned the clean clothes, sheets, and towels to us. The prisoners also did the Coast Guard's laundry.

We had a post office, which, like the canteen, was run by guards, their wives, and their older children, mostly on a volunteer basis. Although mail sent to and by the prisoners was scrutinized and censored, our mail wasn't screened, nor were there any restrictions.

We were not permitted to have "normal" pets, such as cats and dogs; I believe that perhaps we were allowed birds or hamsters, though our family didn't have either.

Taking pictures is a normal thing for families to do, and we did that as well, but not "top side" (at or near the prison). This was forbidden because we would have to be too close to the prison area to get the shots. Also, nearby Angel Island was the site of a Nike missile

Mangle in prison laundry

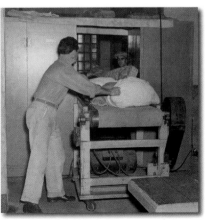

Laundry bags on conveyor belt

Loading produce at the dock

Baking bread

6 DEC 25 MENU 3
CONSOMME
STUFFED CELERY GREEN OLIVES
MIXED SWEET PICKLES
ROAST TOM TURKEY
GIBLET GRAVY CRANBURY SAUCE
CANDIED SWEET POTATOES
RAISIN NUT DRESSING
FRENCH PEAS
WHIPPED POTATOES
HOT APPLE PIE ICE CREAM
BREAD OLEO COFFEE / CR

Steam table in prison dining hall

base. The top of the island's Mt. Livermore had been shaved off to construct a helicopter landing and radar control booth, and missiles were situated underground just below it, aimed and ready to defend the coastline from attack. The Nikes were periodically brought up for drill and testing, and during one of those times, my dad and uncle snapped a picture of them through Dad's telescope.

◇◇◇◇◇◇◇◇◇◇◇◇◇◇◇◇◇◇◇◇◇◇◇◇◇◇◇◇

My parents, just like parents of teenage girls everywhere, had to balance their concern for safety with allowing me the freedom to grow up. There were no police on the island, but there were plenty of guards, and I suppose they served as our police. When it came to safety, we were better protected than people living in cities. All of our criminals were already locked up! And where else but Alcatraz could regular folks rely on high-level security 24/7?

My brother and I were allowed to go to the mainland from time to time when we needed (or wanted) to, to shop, go to the movies or a play, or just meet up with guards' kids who didn't live on the island. Ron, being older than me and male, had more freedom than I did; he went to and from the mainland pretty much at will. I couldn't be in San Francisco alone, so if my mother or someone else wasn't going, Ron was sent along with me. As it turned out, my brother and I went a lot of places together.

There was one thing that was definitely not normal—especially in the life of a teenage girl: using the phone. We didn't talk on the phone because, except for the single telephone booth on the balcony across from the guard tower, the only phones on the island were in the prison. Unlike normal people who had phones in their homes, we had to go down to the phone booth to make a call. We also had to designate a certain time for someone to call us so that we could be sure to be at the telephone when it rang. Although using the phone was anything but convenient, we stayed in touch with friends and relatives this way.

◇◇◇◇◇◇◇◇◇◇◇◇◇◇◇◇◇◇◇◇◇◇◇◇◇◇

To most people, the idea of living close to hard-core criminals was unsettling at least, and this was the aspect of life on the island that many were curious about. People were surprised when I said that living with inmates seemed like no big deal to me. I didn't think much about it, really. I was never afraid.

That is not to say that there were no rules. In fact,

My father's inmate roster also served as his notebook

ROSTER

No.	Name	Detail	Cell
158	Groves, J. *N*	....	*55 YEARS*
248	Waley, H.	....	*45*
325	Karpavicz, A. *ALVIN KARPIS*	....	*LIFE*
		....	*LIFE*
		....	*LIFE*
		....	*LIFE*
		....	*T*
		....	*LIFE*
		....	*T*
		....	*T*
	RDMMAN	....	*LIFE*
		....	*25 Y*
		....	*26 Y - 1 DAY*
		....	*T*
		....	*15 YR*
		....	*LIFE*
		....	*T*
		....	*25 Y*
		....	*20 Y*
		....	*9.8 Y*
	80 JENSEN	....	*10 Y*
	97 LOPEZ	....	*T*
		....	*99 + LIFE*
		....	*25 Y*
		....	*31 Y*
		....	*25 Y*
	T	....	*T*

-4-

UNITED STATES PENITENTIARY

1208
1082

Inmate

ROSTER

Alcatraz, California

44

No.	Name	Detail	Cell
869	Scribner, S.	BROKE MY FINGER	20
871	Mitchell, E.		13
874	Medina, R.		T
			T

No.	Name	Detail	Cell
72	Winhoven, W.	30 YR!	LIFE
76	Fleck, F.	T	15
80	Mayes, H.	T	LIFE
83	Webb, H.	T	LIFE
87	Watson, A.	T	20
89	White, H.	LIFE	20
14	Williams, A.	25 Y	20
18	Williams, J.	T	20
19	Bullock, J.	25	18
22	Brunson, W.	24	30
24	Osborn, F.	LIFE	30
26	McIntyre, D.	23 Y	20
27	Barker, H.	T	T
28	Barker, P.	T	T
32	Kovalik, G.	T	15
40	Stevens, W.	35 Y	15
41	Lawhon, W.	Y T	15
42	Thomas, M.	10 Y Y	25
46	Strickland, H.	T	25
48	Walker, R.	LIFE	0
54	Smith, G.	10 Y Y	16 YR-24 0
56	Fuller, L.	25 Y	18
57	Martin, C.	T	LIFE
58	Smith, J.	30 Y	20
64	Johnson, C.	25	
65	DeNormand, K.	17	
67	Bistram, C.	20	
68	Messamore, W.	28	

No.	Name	Detail	Cell
	Gilford, R.		21 YR - 3 MO
7	Holloman, E.		LIFE
8	Rhodes, W.		& TO 12 YR
9	Steen, L.		LIFE
	McKinney, W.		20 - 26 YR
			20 YR

plenty of precautions were in place. For example, I mentioned that the inmates did our laundry. However, we were told not to send underwear—panties, bras, and so forth—because they either wouldn't come back, or would come back cut up and damaged, or with ink poured on them.

We saw inmates regularly, but only those whose work assignments were outside the cellhouse. Of course, we were forbidden to speak to them when they were working on the dock or collecting the laundry. As a sixteen-year-old girl, I paid more attention to their looks than their circumstances, and found them to be more intriguing than feared.

Once, I got in big trouble for speaking to an inmate. I remember it was summer, because school was out and I was working at the Bank of America as student summer help. That particular day, I was standing on the balcony watching the inmates work on the dock. One of the inmates drifted over close to the balcony and said, "hello," and I said "hello" back. He asked me if I went to school, and I said, "No, school's out. I work." Then he asked, "Where do you work?" I answered matter-of-factly, "The Bank of America." He began to laugh and said, "Oh, don't mention 'bank' to me!" Of course, I didn't know the identities of any of the inmates, but my dad did. I could've been talking to any one of the notorious bank robbers who called Alcatraz home.

About that time, I looked up and spotted Mrs. Latimer, the associate warden's wife, walking across the catwalk. When I saw her, I knew I was in trouble. The next day, I thought I was free and clear because nothing had happened. But then, when my dad got home from work, he told me that he had heard that I was talking to an inmate. He said he knew that I knew that was forbidden, and he really chewed me out! He told me the dangers, reiterated the rules, and then grounded me. For the whole next week, I couldn't go anywhere, even on the weekend. That was the only and last time I spoke to a prisoner!

◇◇◇◇◇◇◇◇◇◇◇◇◇◇◇◇◇◇◇◇◇◇◇◇◇

Like the claim that the *Titanic* was unsinkable, Alcatraz was pegged as escape-proof. Not only did the *Titanic* sink, people did escape from Alcatraz—at least, if you count those who disappeared as escaped. Between 1934 and 1963, there were fourteen official attempts. Of those, some inmates were killed, most were recaptured, and a very few remain "unaccounted for."

Over its twenty-nine-year history, Alcatraz had four

wardens. During the time I lived on the island, Paul Madigan, the third warden, was in charge. On July 23, 1956, Floyd P. Wilson—a murderer serving a life sentence—decided to become the eleventh man to attempt to escape from Alcatraz.

LIFER HUNTED ON ALCATRAZ

Scores of Alcatraz Prison guards continued early today an inch by inch search of the supposedly "escape proof" Rock for a killer inmate missing since yesterday afternoon.

Meanwhile, on the "slim chance" that the vanished convict, 41 year old Floyd Wilson, had somehow slipped ashore, FBI agents were checking the rim of the Bay and police throughout northern California were on the alert.

Missed Check—

Two Coast Guard cutters which had been patroling the island and the Golden Gate were recalled after dark on the theory that if Wilson had reached the water he had long since either drowned or reached shore.

The Washington, D. C., murderer vanished sometime between a line-up check at 3:25 p. m. and a second check twenty minutes later.

The first came—as a routine

(See ESCAPE, Page 20, Col. 5)

FLOYD WILSON
Within 20 Minutes
—Associated Press Wirephoto.

barge had left the dock. Acting Warden J. B. Latimer said he was certain Wilson could not have been aboard either vessel.

The second check was made when the passenger boat returned from San Francisco.

It was then that guards found Wilson missing.

I remember that I was getting ready for a date—I was going to the mainland on the late-afternoon boat. I was standing at my dresser brushing my hair when suddenly, the horns starting blaring. My mother came into my room and told me that we were confined to the island because an inmate had escaped. It was getting late and I knew my date was waiting for me, but there was no way to communicate with him. I later learned that he was very concerned because the dock was chaos.

48

UNITED STATES PENITENTIARY
Alcatraz, California

August 3, 1956

TO: Correctional Office r William G. Burrows

FROM: P. J. Madigan, Warden

RE: Participation in Escape Search

On the occasion of the attempted escape from custody by inmate Floyd P. Wilson on July 23, 1956, it is noted you participated actively in the search according to the hours and positions assigned you by the Acting Captain.

Your cooperation, zealous effort, and willingness to help in a difficult situation such as we faced that night is sincerely appreciated.

Because of the hazards involved and the effort expended by you, it is felt a copy of this memorandum should be placed in your personnel file as a record of cooperation in a difficult situation.

P. J. Madigan
P. J. Madigan,
Warden

In the wee hours of the following morning, Wilson was recaptured. The story is that, while working on the dock, he managed to get about twenty-five feet of cord; his plan was to use the cord to make a raft out of driftwood. When he was missed and the horns were sounded, he decided to hide in a crevice on the rocky shoreline until the guards gave up the search. For twelve hours, he was tossed around in the rocks by the strong current. When found eleven hours later, he was suffering from hypothermia. The warden later wrote my dad a letter, praising him for his help in recapturing the escaped inmate.

The Rocky Road to Love

MR. AND MRS. WILLIS J. PALM
They met "there where the boat comes in"

By Ken McLaughlin

Alcatraz Wedding

Pair Get Life---For Better Or Worse

By James Benet

Ann Burrows, a glowingly pretty 17-year-old, was married here yesterday to Willis J. Palm, 26, also of San Francisco.

As they started on their honeymoon trip to visit his family in Tacoma, Wash., and go on a tour in Can-

ROCK ATTENDANTS

The matron of honor was the bride's aunt, Mrs. John Burrows, whose husband is also a guard—or "custodial officer," as the official title has it—on The Rock.

The best man was her brother, Ronnie, 19.

The Rev. Peter McCormack, the prison's Protestant chaplain, officiated at the ceremonies in the flower-decorated livingroom of the Burrows' apartment. He stood between a doorway and window that both opened onto a spectacu-

on Alcatraz
of some hos
personnel
guards. Yes
tiful sunny
children we
ing each of
ball all ove
balconies a
courtyards 1
any apartmen

The cell b
286 prisoners
worst risks i
tody are "up
a hundred yar
The childre
in the city, con
boat that ma
trips every da
land. Guards
Burrows put in
duty on the boa
towers that co
open spaces or
and part inside
themselves.

Wedding guest
quire formal pas
as they were acc
Burrows as h

guests. But they h
in at the reception
they landed from
and sign out again
ture.

They were not r
go through the te
vice, like a stone
booth open front
which buzzes if the
carrying anything
the visitors to inn
came on the same
carefully sent thro
the registering of
Ann Burrows sa
cial life of a pretty
handicapped by
Alcatraz.

She didn't go
here, because she
high school in Lea
Kan., where her f
been stationed un
transferred to Alc
first of this year.

MODEL WORK

Before that they
Kansas City, Mo., an
some work as a mo
She first met Pa
where the boat co

Dating, Betrothal, Marriage

April 1956

I had been shopping in San Francisco and was waiting for the boat to take me back to the island when I saw a car drive down to the dock, turn around, and then stop. I noticed that it was a nice car and watched as a young man got out. He walked up to me and said that he wanted to ask me a question: why was I was standing around at the dock? I told him that I was going home. He asked where home was and I pointed to the island. That started our conversation.

We talked a while—mostly about the island—the people there, the boat, the schedules. When the *Warden Johnston* arrived and it was time to say good-bye, he realized that he couldn't call me, so he gave me a card with his telephone number. This was how our relationship began, with his curiosity about the island as the catalyst. In the beginning, he seemed to be as interested in the island as he was in me.

The romance blossomed quickly. Only about six months passed between when we met and when we married. During that time, I celebrated my seventeenth

Former Kansas City Model Is Married at Alcatraz

San Francisco, Sept. 30.(AP)—Every time pretty Ann Burrows came home from a date, she came by boat. And a tower guard at Alcatraz had to throw a switch, opening a steel-mesh door.

Yesterday that steel-mesh door opened so that 17-year-old Ann could leave with Willis J. Palm, 26, for Tacoma, Wash., and Canada on their honeymoon.

Ann's father is a guard on the Rock, the island prison in San Francisco bay where the toughest federal prisoners are confined. Ann's family is one of 65 living on Alcatraz.

Ann first met a plumbing supply firm employee, six months ago "right where the boat comes in" at San Francisco from the Rock. They dated frequently, each time requiring recognition from the tower guard when Ann was brought home.

The wedding guests yesterday came by boat—along with friends and kin of the 286 tough convicts. The convicts' visitors had to go through a booth in which a buzzer is set off if the person inspected carries anything metal.

The wedding guests were spared this inspection. But they did have to sign in and out at the reception desk.

The matron of honor was the bride's aunt, whose husband also is a guard on Alcatraz.

The Rock's Protestant chaplain, the Rev. Peter McCormick, performed the ceremony in the Burrows apartment house, built of reinforced concrete five stories high against a cliff.

Ann was given in marriage by her father who was a guard at the federal prison in Leavenworth, Kas., before coming to Alcatraz.

Ann, so pretty she was a model when her family lived in Kansas City, will live with her husband in San Francisco when the honeymoon is over —but in the nearby Marina, within easy boating distance of Alcatraz.

Steel-Mesh Doors Open For Wedding

Bird's eye view of the island

Every Date Was Boat Ride For Couple Wed on Alcatraz

SAN FRANCISCO—(AP)—Every time pretty Ann Burrows came home from a date, she came by boat. And a tower guard at Alcatraz had to throw a switch, opening a steel-mesh door.

birthday. Although my husband-to-be was twenty-six and managed a plumbing supply company, my parents did not approve of my plans, and there were many arguments. But I was persistent and finally, I presented them with an ultimatum: if they didn't agree, I would just run away. Finally, they gave in, on the condition that I finished high school (which I did).

Once the date was set, my mother sent a picture and an announcement of my engagement and wedding plans to the *San Francisco Chronicle* and the *Examiner*. Someone from *Chronicle* contacted my mother, saying that the paper wanted to cover the wedding, and she agreed. On our wedding day, she had to go to the San Francisco dock to meet the reporters, bring them over, and sign them in on the island.

My aunt and my mother planned the wedding. We ordered the cake in San Francisco, and my aunt went to pick it up, along with other things we needed for the wedding. Our apartment wasn't large enough to have both the wedding and the reception in it, and the church wasn't available, so our next-door neighbor agreed to let us have the ceremony in their apartment and we would have the reception in ours.

The ceremony was small—just the immediate

Getting ready for the wedding. Mom, at left; my aunt, at right, in my bedroom.

From left, my brother (the best man), my new husband, me, and my aunt (the matron of honor)

Cutting the cake in my
parents' dining room

After the wedding—getting
off the boat at the Fort
Mason dock

family. Aunt Ilene was the matron of honor, my brother was the best man, and my dad gave me away. The groom's parents lived in Tacoma, Washington. His mother visited my parents before the wedding; his father wasn't well and couldn't make the trip, and they weren't able to attend the wedding. Although like my parents, they were unhappy with us getting married (because of my age), they were nice to me and my family.

The wedding may have been private, but the reception was another story. The whole island, relatives who lived on the mainland, and the press were all invited, and many showed up. The reporters had a lot of questions, and the article ended up being not just about the wedding, but also about me, my new husband, and of course about the island and its residents, both inmates and families. The story appeared in newspapers across the country and even beyond. My mother received thirty or more articles from various newspapers—I remember her getting a congratulatory note from Germany. Just as the island had been the catalyst that began my relationship with my husband, it was also what made an ordinary wedding newsworthy.

We took the 3 p.m. boat to the city and went to the

apartment we had rented. The next day, we headed out for our honeymoon. Our ultimate destination was to be Vancouver, Canada, but on the way we stopped to see relatives in northern California, Oregon, and Washington.

With the wedding over and Alcatraz behind us, I thought we would be just another couple of newlyweds enjoying our honeymoon. However, one night we went out to dinner, and, to my surprise, were recognized from our pictures in the papers. The piano player started playing *Here Comes the Bride.* This was perhaps the first time it really registered with me that I had had the experience of living in a very special place. I felt like a celebrity.

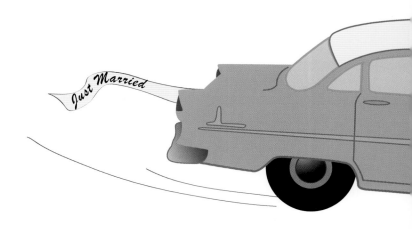

Leaving the Island Behind

San Francisco to Saint Louis, 1957

After the wedding and honeymoon were over, we settled in our apartment in San Francisco. The transition from living with my parents on Alcatraz to married life on the mainland was difficult. While my husband was at work, I felt a bit lonely; I really didn't know what to do with myself. I took care of things in the apartment, but it was small, so when my work was done, I would take the boat to the island and visit with my mom and my aunt.

I think a lot of my difficulty in adjusting had more to do with being married so young than it did with going from life on the island to life on the mainland. I wasn't used to being responsible to (and for) another person; I went from being a carefree teenager to doing housework and having dinner on the table every night. It took several months for me to get acclimated to married life and feel that I was "home." During that time, I felt that home was still on the island. I missed my parents, my bedroom, and my freedom.

I was employed part-time at the bank for about

six months, but quit when I learned that I was pregnant. At first, my aunt would take the boat ride over and we would do things together, such as go to the movies, while my husband and uncle were working. Later, I was so excited about the baby that I no longer thought much about all the adjustments I'd made.

Earlier that year, there had been rumors that Alcatraz was going to close, and my parents, aunt, and uncle decided to leave the island. They were all still fairly young and didn't want to take the chance of being out of work. My father and uncle applied for a variety of jobs; eventually, my dad went back to the Federal Reserve Bank, this time at a branch in St. Louis, Missouri, while my uncle went to work in security with a car company in Indianapolis, Indiana.

When my parents moved back to the Midwest, I became homesick and talked and talked to my husband about following them. My brother Ron had come to live with us for a while, and just before Mike was born in August of 1957, we all made the move to St. Louis. My parents had found an apartment for us not far from where they lived. I didn't work because of the baby, but my husband got a job right away as a report writer for Dun & Bradstreet. I was very glad to be so close to my parents, and although my aunt and uncle were not as near, we still visited frequently, as we had done before.

My brother joined the air force and decided to make a career of it. He also returned to college and got his degree. When my parents moved back to the Midwest, my mom became a full-time housewife and grandmother to Mike and our two daughters, Sharrie Ann, born in 1958, and Karen, born in 1965.

March 1963—the last of the Alcatraz
inmates at the Fort Mason dock

A New Chapter Begins

March 1963 to the Present

Eventually, in 1963, the Bureau of Prisons closed the island penitentiary, transferring the inmates who remained to other institutions. Guards and their families also were transferred, or found other jobs. While its future was being decided, Alcatraz came under the jurisdiction of the federal General Services Administration. In 1969, it was the site of a history-making occupation by young Native American civil-rights activists. During this occupation, four important historic buildings burned to the ground: the warden's house, the lighthouse keeper's quarters, the chief medical technician's house, and the social hall. Once the US Marshals removed the last of the occupiers about nineteen months later, the government tore down the modern apartments (Buildings A, B, and C), and the duplex housing occupied by the associate warden and captain of the guard. Also demolished were the four lieutenants' cottages, all on the family compound around the edges of the parade ground.

By the time the occupation ended in mid-1971, the

movement to bring parks to the people—to set aside land in dense urban areas for national parks—was in full swing. When Golden Gate National Recreation Area was created in 1972, Alcatraz was included within its oversight, placing it under the care of the National Park Service. One year later, it was opened to the public. Today, the "Rock" hosts more than 1.4 million visitors annually.

◇◇◇◇◇◇◇◇◇◇◇◇◇◇◇◇◇◇◇◇◇◇◇◇◇◇◇◇◇◇

In 1967, while the island's eventual use was still in limbo, some of the people who grew up there decided to get together, meeting for a three-day-weekend celebration to socialize and reminisce about the "old days" on Alcatraz. This get-together became an annual event; after several years had gone by, parents were invited to join in. Eventually, all the people who worked or lived on Alcatraz had the opportunity to participate in these reunions. They were a huge success—so much so that the group decided to proclaim itself the Alcatraz Alumni Association (AAA) and include everyone who had ever been connected with the island, including those who could not make the annual event.

In 2006, the association sent a letter to all its members, asking if they would be willing to incorporate the group as a 501(c)(3) nonprofit corporation, which would

Social Hall

make it possible for it to work with GGNRA to heal the wounds suffered by our beloved island. The response was an overwhelming yes, and the group became official.

Two years later, the US Department of the Interior authorized the Alcatraz Alumni Association, Inc., to secure the funding necessary to stabilize the burned-out shell of the former Alcatraz Social Hall. The AAA is currently engineering the stabilization of the structure to prevent the shell from collapsing. The association hopes to be allowed to rebuild the Social Hall as its own Alcatraz Alumni Museum to house and display members' collections related to Alcatraz history as well as a classroom for troubled youth. The AAA also hopes to restore the landmark lighthouse.

Me today

With Phil at the reunion

Ann of Alcatraz, fifty years later

August 2007

I attended my first Alcatraz Alumni Association celebration in August 2007. Some of the members had set up booths, where they visited with the tourists, displayed pictures, answered questions, and even gave autographs. As I was on my way to the parade ground with my son and his wife, Annette, I saw a booth with the name Phil Dollison. Immediately I recognized the name as "the" Phil I knew and even dated for a bit while I lived on the island. I grabbed Annette's arm and told her who he was. I was shy, but she urged me to go talk to him.

I'm glad I did, because it was a wonderful meeting. He didn't recognize me right away (it had been fifty years, after all!) but he certainly remembered when I told him this story. "You wanted a motorcycle and your dad wouldn't let you have it. We assessed the situation and decided that if you stayed in one of the garages and didn't let your parents know where you were, it would worry them and then, when you came home, they would be so relieved they would let you have a motorcycle."

Phil and I at the Tonga Room, San Francisco

Phil and his motorcycle

At this point, Phil chimed in and continued the tale: "My girlfriend—you—knocked on the garage door and told me that my mother was upset and crying and to call her."

"Yes," I said. "Some of the kids and I went to your house—I can't remember why—and your mom told me she didn't know where you were, and burst into tears. That got to my heart, so I told her not to worry—I would gather some of the kids and we'd find you. That's when I went straight to the garage and told you to call your mom."

He got the motorcycle. For his first trip, he picked me up on the dock in San Francisco and we went to the beach for the day. I don't think our parents knew we were on the bike.

After exchanging stories, he gave me a big hug. The kids took a picture and were as excited as we were. Although we didn't get to talk much the rest of the day, we exchanged phone numbers and email addresses and have been in touch regularly since.

Although it seemed perfectly normal and mundane at the time, I now realize that spending my teen years on Alcatraz was a very special experience. It not only shaped my young years, it carried through my entire

life, creating a common bond with others that has lasted for fifty years.

Like all of those who remember the island the way it was when our families lived there, I would love to see the damaged buildings restored and its stories survive beyond those who remember it firsthand. It is an honor to be able to contribute to the pursuit of preserving Alcatraz by sharing my personal memories in pictures and writing. It is a privilege to have been part of history.

Suggested Reading

Over the years, many books have been written and films have been made about Alcatraz and its history. Former inmates, correctional officers, people who grew up on the island, scholars who've studied its various eras: taken together, their stories weave a vivid historical tapestry. Following is a sampling of works that will deepen your understanding of the island and its place in history.

Alcatraz Reunion (DVD). Directed by John Paget. Paget Films, 2009.

Babyak, Jolene. *Eyewitness on Alcatraz.* Oakland, CA: Ariel Vamp Press, 1988.

Esslinger, Michael. *Alcatraz: A Definitive History of the Penitentiary Years.* Carmel, CA: Ocean View Publishing, 2003.

Johnson, Troy. *We Hold the Rock: The Indian Occupation of Alcatraz 1969-1971.* San Francisco: Golden Gate National Parks Conservancy, 1997. (See also the documentary, *Alcatraz Is Not an Island.* For more information, go to *www.pbs.org/ itvs/alcatrazisnotanisland/*)

Lageson, Ernest (Sr. & Jr.). *Guarding the Rock: A Father and Son Remember Alcatraz.* San Francisco: Golden Gate National Parks Conservancy, 2008.

Martini, John A. *Alcatraz at War.* San Francisco: Golden Gate National Parks Conservancy, 2002.

Murphy, Claire Rudolf. *Children of Alcatraz: Growing Up on the Rock.* New York: Walker Books, 2006.

Odier, Pierre. *The Rock: A History of Alcatraz, the Fort, the Prison.* Eagle Rock, CA: L'Image Odier, 1983.

Quillen, Jim. *Alcatraz from Inside: The Hard Years 1942-1952.* San Francisco: Golden Gate National Parks Conservancy, 1991.

Ward, David. *Alcatraz: The Gangster Years.* Berkeley: University of California Press, 2010.

These books are available on Alcatraz. Please call (415) 561-4922.

NATIONAL PARK SERVICE

The National Park Service (NPS) was created in 1916 to preserve America's natural, cultural, and scenic treasures. The NPS manages the Golden Gate National Recreation Area (commonly known as the Golden Gate National Parks) as well as more than 390 other national park sites across the country.

THE GOLDEN GATE NATIONAL PARKS

Extending in all directions from San Francisco's Golden Gate is a vast collection of national parks. A rich blend of natural and historic sites, the Golden Gate National Parks preserve a variety of splendid landscapes, precious habitats, and important landmarks. Best of all, these parks are on the doorstep of the San Francisco Bay Area. Discover some of the country's most beautiful places, the Golden Gate National Parks.

www.nps.gov/goga   *www.nps.gov/alcatraz*

GOLDEN GATE NATIONAL PARKS CONSERVANCY

The Golden Gate National Parks Conservancy is the nonprofit membership organization created to preserve the Golden Gate National Parks, enhance the experiences of park visitors, and build a community dedicated to conserving the parks for the future. To become a member and learn more, visit *www.parksconservancy.org.*

Your Purchase Supports the Parks